MW00586978

The Holy of Holies

Discovering What the Bible Says About the Dwelling
Place of God

Logan Wolf

Sermon To Book
www.sermontobook.com

The Holy of Holies / Logan Wolf
ISBN-13: 978-1-952602-08-5

The Holy of Holies is a comprehensive look at the role, function, and purpose of God's temple from inception to today. This will help anyone gain a greater clarity as to why the physical temple was important under the Old Covenant and how God has, in the New Covenant, transitioned the role of the temple into a spiritual one because of Christ's total fulfillment of the law by his perfect once and for all sacrifice. Logan has made this both theologically rich and practical.

Nate Fox | Executive Director, Elevation Project, Associate Lead Pastor, Lifestone Church

To Utah, a people and a place I love.

CONTENTS

More Than Stone and Mortar

Temple is a word seldom used in modern Christianity, which is interesting, considering how often temples are mentioned in the Bible. Christians today tend to associate temples with ancient cultures, like the Greeks or Egyptians, or even other faiths, such as Hinduism or Buddhism. In fact, I am writing this in Utah, a state dotted with seventeen Mormon temples.

Derived from the Latin word *templum*, which refers to a raised platform dedicated to sacred purposes, *temple* is a general term for any location where worship or service to a deity takes place.[1] We see a variety of temples in the Bible. There is the temple of Dagon at Ashdod (1 Samuel 5:2), a pagan temple where King Saul's head was displayed after he was killed; the temple of the calves at Bethel (1 Kings 12:31–33); the temple of Rimmon at Damascus (2 Kings 5:18); the temple of Baal at Samaria (2 Kings 10:21); the temple of Merodach, or Mars, in Babylon (2 Chronicles 36:7); and the temple of Diana, or Artemis, at Ephesus (Acts 19:27), which Paul denounced, causing a riot among those who worshiped the pagan goddess. Of course, the temple that should receive most of our attention is the one constructed in Jerusalem by the Israelites to worship the one true God, as well as its temporary predecessor, the tabernacle.

Pages upon pages of the Old Testament are devoted to the intricate instructions given for building and maintaining both the tabernacle and the temple, with specifications for everything from the embroidery on the curtains to the weight of the metal utensils to be used at the altar. In contrast, Christians today gather in all sorts of places, from living rooms, elementary school cafeterias, storefronts, and movie theaters to more traditional church buildings with pulpits, choir lofts, and stained-glass windows. The choice of location seems more mindful of practicality than direct instruction from God.

Have we missed something? Has something been lost? Absolutely not. We've gained more than the Israelites ever could have imagined! Because of the new covenant ushered in by Jesus and the Holy Spirit in us, we can worship in the fullness of God's presence anywhere, as we'll see.

What, then, is the purpose of our taking time to understand the biblical idea of the temple? The temple, along with the rules and traditions surrounding it, received so much ink in the Old Testament because it was important to God and His people. Even if we are freer today in our perception of what makes an appropriate place of worship, we are wise to pay attention to the biblical temple stories because of what they can teach us about God Almighty and His pursuit of us.

Delving into the importance of the temple in the lives of Moses, Solomon, Jesus, and the early Church, we will see the doors to our own hearts opened as we learn more about the One whom we worship. And there is another vital reason for us to learn everything we can about this biblical idea of a temple: *we* are temples, too. First Corinthians 6:19–20 tells us:

> *What? know ye not that your body is the temple of the Holy Ghost which is in you, which ye have of God, and ye are not your own? For ye are bought with a price: therefore glorify God in your body, and in your spirit, which are God's.*

In his first letter to the Corinthians, Paul reframed the idea of the temple. From this metaphor, we understand that the temple is more than stone and mortar, that every Christian becomes the dwelling place of God the Spirit. Our understanding of this temple will govern both how we live as believers and how we relate to the God who inspires our worship.

As you prepare your heart to enter the rich world of the biblical temple, pray for new insights into ancient truths. At the end of each chapter, reflection questions will help you to articulate those insights and apply them to your everyday life.

The journey that awaits us on our temple tour is highlighted by reminders of God's love and care for His people, as well as His justice and holiness. Ultimately, it is the temple in the New Testament that vividly illustrates the new life we can embrace as followers of Christ. With this in mind, let's pull back the heavy, lavish curtain, step into the first temple, and begin our journey.

CHAPTER ONE

In Our Midst:
Moses and the Tabernacle

To grasp the importance of the layout and practices of the early temple, you must go back to the very beginning of man's relationship with God. The Bible opens with God creating the world and the masterpiece of His creation, mankind (Genesis 1). God desired to have a special relationship with mankind, one in which He provided for all of man's needs and man found satisfaction and fulfillment in God.

To that end, God gave Adam and Eve, the first man and woman, a choice by planting two special trees, the Tree of Life and the Tree of the Knowledge of Good and Evil. Adam and Eve were permitted to eat of the Tree of Life. By doing so, they would acknowledge God as their source of life. However, they were forbidden to eat of the Tree of the Knowledge of Good and Evil. By not doing so, they would express their dependence on God for truth and direction. God warned Adam that to eat of that tree would bring punishment: death.

Prior to the creation of the world, God made the angels (Job 38:4–7). One of those angels, Lucifer, was cast out of heaven because of his aspirations to be like God (Isaiah 14:14). Lucifer's hatred for God led to his hatred for mankind. He looked to destroy the relationship Adam and Eve had with God. Disguised as a serpent, Lucifer approached Eve and, by deception, convinced her to disobey God and eat of the fruit from the Tree of the Knowledge of Good and Evil. She, in turn, offered some of the fruit to Adam. Adam, to whom God had explicitly given the command not to eat of the fruit from the tree, made a conscious decision to disobey.

This opportunity revealed what was already going on in Adam's heart and mind. He wanted to determine for himself what was good and evil, what was true. He wanted to be his own authority. When Adam rebelled against God in this way, sin was introduced into the world, and everything that God had said would happen did happen. Mankind became subject to physical death and immediately experienced spiritual death because their sin created a chasm between them and God.

As head of the human race, Adam represented each of us. We've inherited this broken relationship with God and Adam's sinful nature (Romans 5:12). Isaiah 59:2 reads, "But your iniquities have separated between you and your God, and your sins have hid his face from you, that he will not hear." That chasm still exists.

Though mankind has been unfaithful to God, looking for satisfaction and fulfillment elsewhere, He remains faithful to each of us. He has provided a Deliverer to overcome our sin and reconcile us to Himself. That Deliverer came when God sent His Son, Jesus, to earth to die for our sins as a substitute. However, before that time, men and women lived in anticipation of this Deliverer, foreshadowed through the ritual of animal sacrifice.

These sacrifices took place in the tabernacle, first mentioned in Exodus 20, after Moses led the Israelites out of slavery in Egypt and God gave him the Ten Commandments. Finally, after so many years of slavery, God's people were free to worship. God gave Moses specific guidelines for the creation of the temporary temple, or tabernacle, that would provide a place for worship as they journeyed.

The Lord told Moses:

> Ye shall not make with me gods of silver, neither shall ye make unto you gods of gold. An altar of earth thou shalt make unto me, and shalt sacrifice thereon thy burnt offerings, and thy peace offerings, thy sheep, and thine oxen: in all places where I record my name I will come unto thee, and I will bless thee.
>
> **—Exodus 20:23–24**

Because of the human sin condition and the fact that God's holiness and our sinfulness cannot coexist, the tabernacle had to provide necessary accommodations to allow the Israelites to worship God despite their inability to commune directly with Him.

The Tabernacle Provided Separation

The tabernacle consisted of three sections. The outer area, the courtyard, was surrounded by a tall linen curtain, and the Israelites entered through a thirty-foot entrance on the east side. The courtyard was a large, busy place, full of priests bustling about and a variety of animals that would be offered on the altar as sacrifices (Exodus 38:9–20).

From the courtyard, priests could enter the tabernacle itself, which stood fifteen feet tall and consisted of the Holy Place and the Holy of Holies. The Holy Place contained three important items: the golden lampstand, which provided the primary light within the tabernacle, the table holding the consecrated loaves of shewbread (or showbread), and the altar of incense (Exodus 35:10–19).

Behind the altar was an elaborate veil, which, according to Moses' instructions, was to be created from the best blue, purple, and scarlet thread and emblazoned with cherubim. The veil was hung from four tall wooden posts, which were covered in gold and stood on bases of silver, and it formed the separation between the Holy Place and the Holy of Holies, where the Spirit of God Himself dwelled.

The Holy of Holies was fifteen by fifteen feet, and the only piece of furniture in the sacred chamber was the Ark of the Covenant. God manifested His presence above the lid of the Ark, which was called the mercy seat. The mercy seat was made of solid gold and depicted a cherub on each end, covering the mercy seat with its wings.

The only person who could enter the Holy of Holies was the high priest, and he could only enter on one day a year, the Day of Atonement. It was believed that anyone else who entered would die because he or she would be unable to stand in the presence of the holy God. The veil between the Holy Place and the Holy of Holies was a vivid reminder of the divide between God and man that was first formed in the Garden of Eden (Genesis 3:24) and deepened with the sin of each generation.

The latter part of the book of Exodus is full of particular instructions for constructing the tabernacle. The Israelites, directed by Moses, followed those directions to the letter, creating a space where God could be glorified and worshiped. After the completion of the tabernacle, God dwelled in the midst of His people:

> Then a cloud covered the tent of the congregation, and the glory of the LORD filled the tabernacle. And Moses was not able to enter into the tent of the congregation, because the cloud abode thereon, and the glory of the LORD filled the tabernacle.
>
> **—Exodus 40:34–35**

The tabernacle pleased God, and it was filled with His glory, but man's sinful heart meant that even a man like Moses could not enter and experience God's glory up close.

The Tabernacle Provided Mediation

The issue of man's sinfulness required more than physical separation for the process of worshiping God; it also necessitated a mediator between the Israelites and God. Of the twelve tribes of Israel, the tribe of Levi had set itself apart with its faithfulness to God and devotion to worship. So, God set apart the Levites for a holy purpose, designating them as the priests in the tabernacle. The Levites were held to a high standard because of their important calling, as is illustrated in Numbers 8:5–26, where God gave a series of detailed instructions for their purification. As priests and servants in the tabernacle, they had to be cleansed with holy water, shaved all over their bodies, and consecrated with a special offering of bulls.

The Levites had a host of responsibilities, including maintaining the tabernacle and ensuring that everything was prepared for worship. One group of Levites, those directly descended from Aaron, served as priests, while others in the tribe carried out other duties. Later, after the permanent temple was completed, Levites also provided the music. Aaron was the first high priest, and so he was the first to make an offering inside the Holy of Holies. Subsequent high priests came from his line. The high priest wore elaborate priestly garments, oversaw the other priests, and fulfilled his most important duty on the Day of Atonement.

At this time, you had to be born into the tribe of Levi to serve, and you had to claim the lineage of Aaron to become a priest. In Numbers 3:6, the Lord told Moses, "Bring the tribe of Levi near, and present them before

Aaron the priest, that they may minister unto him." In verse 10, God said, "And thou shalt appoint Aaron and his sons, and they shall wait on their priest's office: and the stranger that cometh nigh shall be put to death."

God made it clear that the Levites would be set apart for His service, but their role wasn't purely ceremonial. The priests were essential if the Israelites were to maintain a relationship with God because, at that time, the people required a mediator to get to God.

The Tabernacle Provided Sanctification

One of the principal purposes of the tabernacle was to provide a way for the people to be sanctified, or made holy. God both demands and grants holiness, and He designed the tabernacle and the sacrificial system that would allow His people to achieve sanctification for their sins. As God explained in Leviticus 17:11, "For the life of the flesh is in the blood: and I have given it to you upon the altar to make an atonement for your souls: for it is the blood that maketh an atonement for the soul." As we read in Hebrews 9:22, "without shedding of blood is no remission."

Because God desired that His people be sanctified, He established the annual Day of Atonement, on which the high priest made a sacrifice to seek cleansing for all the sins of the people. The high priest sprinkled blood on the bronze altar within the tabernacle courtyard and then entered the Holy of Holies to sprinkle more blood on the mercy seat.

Leviticus 16 details the elaborate ritual Aaron went through every year to atone for the sins of the Israelites. In Leviticus 16:33, the Lord instructed of the high priest, "he shall make an atonement for the holy sanctuary, and he shall make an atonement for the tabernacle of the congregation, and for the altar, and he shall make an atonement for the priests, and for all the people of the congregation." This act of atonement achieved reconciliation between the Lord and His people, but the barrier between them was only temporarily removed.

Even though the atonement sacrifice was important in the Israelites' worship of God, it was not an end in itself, but rather a foreshadowing of the Savior who was promised. As Hebrews 10:4 reminds us, "it is not possible that the blood of bulls and of goats should take away sins." Animal sacrifices reminded the people that their sins were costly and that blood must be shed for reconciliation to occur, and this picture of death pointed forward to the One who would remove the sin barrier once and for all. The tabernacle was vital in providing sanctification and setting the stage for the true Lamb of God who was to come.

A Reminder

The tabernacle, the first temple constructed according to God's design, is a reminder of God's desire to dwell among His people. It made accommodations for a holy God and sinful man to coexist. It provided separation by way of the veil, it provided mediation by way of the priests, and it provided sanctification by way of the sacrifices. It was a step toward the ideal found in Genesis of man and God walking together and living in relationship. However, it was not the final step. All the beauty and ceremony found in the tabernacle was simply "a shadow of good things to come" (Hebrews 10:1).

God's desire to dwell among His people hasn't changed, but the expression of that desire did change with the death of Christ. Under the new covenant, the Lord has gone from manifesting His presence in the tabernacle to living among us in the form of the Holy Spirit, without the need for physical separation, human mediation, or blood sacrifice. Because of Christ, the ideal first set forth in the Garden of Eden—man walking in fellowship with his Creator—is possible again. Christ has made a way for us.

This truth is expressed in Matthew 1:23: "Behold, a virgin shall be with child, and shall bring forth a son, and they shall call his name Emmanuel, which being interpreted is, God with us." We no longer have to go to the tabernacle to meet with God. We can meet with Him anywhere—at church, in the kitchen, as we are driving to work, out in nature—through our permanent Mediator and Deliverer, Jesus Christ.

Praise God that Jesus became our Mediator and opened the way so that we could have a relationship with our Heavenly Father. As we read in Hebrews, the Israelites served as an "example and shadow of heavenly things" (Hebrews 8:5), a shadow of a better reality we now have in the completed work of Jesus Christ.

Chapter One Questions

Question: Why was physical separation from God a necessary component of worship in ancient Israel (under the old covenant)?

_____

_____

_____

_____

_____

_____

_____

_____

_____

_____

_____

Question: Which tribe facilitated worship at the tabernacle (and later the temple)? Why were they chosen? (Read Exodus 32 for additional insight.) Describe their priestly duties.

_____

_____

_____

_____

_____

_____

_____

_____

_____

_____

_____

Question: What happened on the Day of Atonement? What was the purpose of animal sacrifices, and what did they foreshadow?

_____

_____

_____

_____

_____

_____

_____

_____

_____

_____

_____

_____

Action: Read Hebrews 9–10 in light of the information in this chapter. Make a table contrasting ministry at the earthly tabernacle and the heavenly tabernacle. Note any new insights you gain about Jesus, our Mediator, and respond in prayer.

_____

_____

_____

_____

_____

_____

_____

_____

CHAPTER TWO

The House of the Lord: Solomon and the Temple

The tabernacle might have been temporary, but for many generations of Israelites, it was the only place of worship they ever knew. The people of God worshiped in the tabernacle, which moved with them through the wilderness and brought them into the Promised Land, for 485 years. The tabernacle was the center of worship under the leadership of Moses, of Joshua, and finally, after the Israelites had taken the land promised to them so many years earlier, of King David.

When David became king, he grew unsettled by the fact that God's presence was housed in a temporary tabernacle while he resided in a grand palace. Called "a man after mine [God's] own heart" (Acts 13:22), David yearned to honor God's majesty by creating a place of worship worthy of Him. In 1 Chronicles 17:1, he told the prophet Nathan, "Lo, I dwell in an house of cedars, but the ark of the covenant of the LORD remaineth under curtains."

David resolved to do something about the situation, and he told God that he desired to build a permanent temple to house the Ark of the Covenant and to provide a place of worship and sacrifice. Even though David's goal was a worthy one, God made it clear that David was not the one who had been chosen to build the temple. God said to Nathan, "Go and tell David my servant, Thus saith the LORD, Thou shalt not build me an house to dwell in" (1 Chronicles 17:4). God told David through Nathan that his son Solomon would be given the job when the crown passed to him: "I will raise up thy seed after thee, which shall be of thy sons; and I will establish his kingdom. He shall build me an house, and I will stablish his throne for ever" (1 Chronicles 17:11–12).

The temple would fulfill the same purposes as the tabernacle—providing separation, mediation, and sanctification—but Solomon's elaborate plans and process to construct it underscored the importance of the structure and its mission. At a time when the Israelites were beginning to grow complacent and forget all that God had done for them when they left Egypt and claimed the Promised Land, the temple served to reaffirm God's role in their lives and their nation.

The Temple Reaffirmed God's Promise

Solomon put everything he had into the construction of the temple. In 2 Chronicles 2:2, we learn that he recruited 70,000 men to carry supplies, 80,000 to quarry rock, and

3,600 to oversee the sizable crew. He paid attention to every detail of the construction, including the creation of ten golden lampstands, ten tables, and a hundred basins of gold (2 Chronicles 4:7–19). No expense was spared, and every detail was important. Finally, when all was completed, Solomon ordered the elders to bring the Ark of the Covenant and set it in its place in the Holy of Holies, and the king gathered the Israelites together for a dedication ceremony.

The dedication of the grand worship space moved Solomon's spirit, inspiring him to praise God in the longest recorded prayer in the Bible (1 Kings 8:22–53). Solomon was struck by God's faithfulness, both to his father and to him, and by God's fulfillment of His promise to complete the temple in Solomon's reign. In 1 Kings 8:23–24, Solomon said to the Lord, "There is no God like thee, … Who hast kept with thy servant David my father that thou promisedst him: thou spakest also with thy mouth, and hast fulfilled it with thine hand, as it is this day."

God was clear, during David's reign, that He planned to hold off on the temple construction until David had died and Solomon had become king. Even if David wasn't to oversee the building himself, he held fast to God's promises of the future temple and anticipated the fulfillment of those promises. Like his son, he worshiped God and thanked Him for His faithfulness, praying, "Therefore now, LORD, let the thing that thou hast spoken concerning thy servant and concerning his house be estab-lished for ever" (1 Chronicles 17:23). God permitted David to make preparations for the temple, and David was given the responsibility of buying the parcel of land where the temple would eventually be built, a threshing floor that belonged to a Jebusite man and was located on Mount Moriah.

The location of the plot of land gave God's promise and its fulfillment even greater significance. It was to Mount Moriah that God led Abraham in Genesis 22:1–14 and asked him to do the unthinkable, to sacrifice his son Isaac. Abraham resolved to obey, trusting that God knew something he didn't. As he raised the knife, I imagine there was heartache, sadness, and confusion. Isaac was a cherished baby given to Abraham and Sarah late in life, and he was the one through whom God's promise to multiply Abraham's descendants was to be fulfilled. Were Isaac to die, God's promise to restore mankind to Himself would die with him. But God provided a substitute, a ram caught by its horns in a thicket nearby.

What better place than Mount Moriah could David have possibly chosen to represent God's faithfulness through the generations? Just as He had provided a way for Abraham and made him the father of Israel, He would bless the temple that would stand in that spot to give glory to Himself, the ultimate Promise Keeper. Even when tragedy eventually befell the temple, God's faithfulness toward His children remained through every generation, ultimately leading Him to send His Son as the permanent substitute for temporary temple sacrifices.

David might not have been able to see the completed temple, but he was involved enough to know how the project would turn out. He even gave Solomon the detailed plans for the structure, telling his son, "Be strong and of good courage, and do it: fear not, nor be dismayed: for the LORD God, even my God, will be with thee; he will not fail thee, nor forsake thee, until thou hast finished all the work for the service of the house of the LORD" (1 Chronicles 28:20).

The Temple Reaffirmed God's Preeminence

Solomon would need to recall his father's reminder to be strong and courageous because the construction of the temple would be taxing in terms of time, effort, and resources. Though the temple included the same divisions and furniture as the tabernacle, everything was constructed on a much grander scale. At today's value, the gold alone used in the temple would be worth nearly $141.5 billion.[2] Even with a workforce of more than 100,000 men, the temple took seven years to construct.

The temple was finally completed in 960 BC, prompting an elaborate festival, at which Solomon prayed his prayer of dedication. During that fourteen-day feast, Solomon offered 22,000 oxen and 120,000 sheep to the Lord to commemorate the occasion (2 Chronicles 7:5). Despite the scope and grandeur of the temple project, Solomon spoke a vital truth as he prayed: that no earthly building could ever contain or compare to the power and majesty of God. In 1 Kings 8:27, Solomon asked, "But will God indeed dwell on the earth? behold, the heaven and heaven of heavens cannot contain thee; how much less this house that I have builded?"

Solomon understood that God is preeminent; He is supreme and exalted above His creation. The temple was big, but God is bigger still. The temple might have included $141.5 billion worth of gold, but all the gold in the world belongs to God. Solomon didn't confuse the physical representation of God's presence with God Himself. He knew that God's presence is never limited or confined to buildings constructed with human hands. That was wisdom he had gained from a young age because his father, David, also understood the true preeminence of God Almighty.

In Psalm 68:34–35, David wrote, "Ascribe ye strength unto God: his excellency is over Israel, and his strength is in the clouds. O God, thou art terrible out of thy holy places: the God of Israel is he that giveth strength and power unto his people. Blessed be God." David and Solomon wanted the temple to give God the glory He is due, but they understood that God could display His power and might in any way and in any place that He chose.

The Temple Reaffirmed God's Purity

The completion of the temple was cause for celebration for Solomon and the Israelites. At long last, they had a permanent place to worship and sacrifice to God. But the chasm between God and man was just as wide and impossible to cross as it had been when the tabernacle was constructed. Because of sin, true fellowship between broken man and holy God couldn't be achieved even with the grandest of buildings and the most elaborate of rituals.

As in the tabernacle, the sacrifices in the temple had to be made repeatedly. In 1 Kings 8:30, Solomon asked God to forgive the people for a host of sins, but he knew as he prayed that the people would continue to commit such offenses and, therefore, the temple would continue to be a place where man sacrificed animals in hopes that he could be right with God.

Numbers 6:14 gives just a taste of the detailed instructions the Israelites had to observe to achieve this temporary peace with God:

> *And he shall offer his offering unto the LORD, one he lamb of the first year without blemish for a burnt offering, and one ewe lamb of the first year without blemish for a sin offering, and one ram without blemish for peace offerings.*

The people made sacrifices in the temple courtyard, and the priests made their ritual sacrifices inside the temple, just as they had in the tabernacle.

The basin in the courtyard, called the brazen sea, held 17,000 gallons of water used for the ritual cleansing of priests before and after offering sacrifices.[3] Next to the brazen sea stood the brazen altar, which was more than three times the size of the corresponding altar in the tabernacle. The temple was a larger, grander reminder of God's purity and the people's inability to measure up to His holiness. Every time the people worshiped a golden calf, complained about God's provision, or intermarried with pagans who worshiped false idols, the distance between God and His chosen people seemed to widen.

Even as His people sought to offer the right types of animals for specific holy days or certain purposes and to make those sacrifices over and over again, God knew that

He was preparing a better way. God's perfect plan was in place, and soon He would reveal a new covenant that would allow His people to enter His presence without animal blood or the fear of death. The animal sacrifices that took place in the temple were a reminder that sin could be paid for only by the shedding of blood. They served as a graphic picture of the death sin deserves and pointed forward to the promised Deliverer, who would overcome sin once and for all. By fulfilling the sacrifices, the Israelites were acknowledging their sin and God's purity and expressing their trust in God's promise.

A Promise

The temple was another step toward the ideal that had been left behind in Genesis, but it wasn't the final step. The construction of the temple reaffirmed what we have already seen in the tabernacle. It reaffirmed God's promise, first to David about the construction of the temple and then to mankind to send a Deliverer who would overcome sin and death. It reaffirmed His preeminence, the fact that God transcends His creation and is not confined to buildings. And it reaffirmed the truth that God, in His purity and holiness, cannot ignore the sinfulness of man.

The temple wasn't an end in itself; it couldn't defeat sin. However, like the tabernacle, it did point forward to the One who would. The temple was another picture, or shadow (Hebrews 10:1), of the promised Deliverer, Jesus Christ.

In Romans 8:1–30, we gain a clearer understanding of God's purpose in sending His Son to restore the broken relationship between God and man. People who had strived for thousands of years to find a way into God's presence suddenly gained freedom through grace to know the almighty God and even to be called children of God and co-heirs with Christ (Romans 8:15–27). We can rejoice in this truth:

> There is therefore now no condemnation to them which are in Christ Jesus, who walk not after the flesh, but after the Spirit. For the law of the Spirit of life in Christ Jesus hath made me free from the law of sin and death. For what the law could not do, in that it was weak through the flesh, God sending his own Son in the likeness of sinful flesh, and for sin, condemned sin in the flesh.
> —*Romans 8:1–3*

Today we don't have to go to a temple to meet with God; we meet with Him through Jesus Christ. It is Christ who sanctifies us through His blood. He has become our Mediator, having made a way, through grace alone, for us to enter into a relationship with God and come boldly into His presence.

Chapter Two Questions

Question: What was the significance of the site for the temple? How does the story in Genesis 22 foreshadow Christ?

_____

_____

_____

_____

_____

_____

_____

_____

_____

_____

Question: Solomon didn't confuse the physical represen-
tation of God's presence with God Himself. What are
some ways people today sometimes look to objects or
buildings instead of the person and presence of Christ
Himself?

_____

_____

_____

_____

_____

_____

_____

_____

_____

_____

_____

Question: What does the grandeur of Solomon's temple
teach us about God? What does it say about David and
Solomon? Is it important for believers today to meet in
impressive buildings? Why or why not?

_____

_____

_____

_____

_____

_____

_____

_____

_____

_____

_____

_____

Action: Read Solomon's beautiful prayer of dedication in 1 Kings 8:22–53 and 2 Chronicles 6:12–42. Write down five principles you can learn from the structure and content of this prayer and apply them to your own prayer life.

_____

_____

_____

_____

_____

_____

_____

_____

_____

CHAPTER THREE

Torn in Two:
Jesus and the Temple

At long last, King Solomon had the opportunity to preside over the construction of the temple on Mount Moriah. The dedication of the grand, sacred worship place was surely one of his proudest moments on the throne. But the euphoria and unity prompted by the temple's completion wouldn't long outlive Solomon himself (2 Chronicles 3–9).

After Solomon died, Israel was split into two separate kingdoms: the northern kingdom of Israel and the southern kingdom of Judah (2 Chronicles 10; 1 Kings 12). The unrest caused by God's people dividing into two separate kingdoms contributed to several hundred years of sinful rebellion, political upheaval, and divine judgment. The situation was so tumultuous that the armies of Judah began pillaging the temple, originally designed to be the symbol of God's power and holiness, in an effort to secure allies for themselves.

Their sin would be dealt with in 586 BC, when King Nebuchadnezzar and his Babylonian army seized Jerusalem, burned the temple and the rest of the city, and led the people away to captivity in Babylon. This chaotic scene is described in 2 Kings 25:8–9:

> *And in the fifth month, ... came Nebuzaradan, captain of the guard, a servant of the king of Babylon, unto Jerusalem: And he burnt the house of the LORD, and the king's house, and all the houses of Jerusalem, and every great man's house burnt he with fire.*

Eventually, the Persians overthrew the Babylonians, and a Persian king named Cyrus allowed the Jews to reconstruct the temple. This second version of the temple, which was considerably less grand than Solomon's temple, was completed in 515 BC. The most obvious omission from the new temple was inside the Holy of Holies, which stood empty. The sacred Ark of the Covenant had disappeared during the Babylonian destruction of Solomon's temple.[4]

After nearly 350 years without incident, the new temple was plundered by the Seleucids in 170 BC. One hundred years after that, Rome took control of Jerusalem under King Herod. In an effort to gain favor with his new subjects, Herod authorized an enormous renovation project of the temple, which had been ravaged by time and repeated assaults. This massive facelift, which began in 20 BC and was completed in AD 64, doubled the size of the temple and added impressive gates, porches, and courts. All that remains today of Herod's expanded temple is the "Wailing Wall," a holy site in Jerusalem.[5]

This renovated temple was the place where Jewish people worshiped at the time of Christ's birth. Much of what we know of Jesus' life took place in and around the temple: His circumcision as an infant (Luke 2:22–38), His trip to the temple to observe Passover (when He was accidentally left there by His family) at age 12 (Luke 2:41–50), and the many instances when He taught and healed at the temple throughout His public ministry. In the final week of His life, Jesus even overturned tables and drove out money changers in the temple because the holy place of worship had been corrupted by commercial pursuits (Matthew 21:12–13).

Christ enraged Jewish leaders when He said, "I will destroy this temple that is made with hands, and within three days I will build another made without hands" (Mark 14:58). This was an outrageous claim to the Pharisees and other religious leaders of the day, and it eventually led to Jesus' unjust trial and crucifixion. Ironically, in demanding the Savior's death, the leaders helped to ensure the fulfillment of God's promise to reconcile mankind to Himself and eliminate the need for the temple. Christ Himself would become our temple by fulfilling the purposes of the Old Testament tabernacle and temple.

Jesus Eliminated Our Separation

All of us were born with the same sin nature, the same spiritual problem, which originated with the disobedience of Adam. We read in Romans 5:12, "Wherefore, as by one man sin entered into the world, and death by sin; and so death passed upon all men, for that all have sinned." Earlier in Romans, we learn that we are part of a blanket indictment: "For all have sinned, and come short of the glory of God" (Romans 3:23). In Isaiah 53:6, we are compared to sheep that "have gone astray."

Our sin separates us from God, and examples of this estrangement are found throughout the Old Testament: Adam and Eve being expelled from the Garden of Eden (Genesis 3:23), God asking Moses to draw a boundary at the base of Mount Sinai (Exodus 19:23), and the veil separating the Holy Place from the Holy of Holies, first in the tabernacle and later in the temple (Exodus 26:33). The veil served as a constant reminder that sinful man is unable to approach a holy God. We read in Isaiah 59:2, "But your iniquities have separated between you and your God, and your sins have hid his face from you, that he will not hear."

Only through animal sacrifices—temporary measures governed by extensive rules—could God's people achieve even a temporary experience of atonement. The fact that the Israelites had to return to the temple carrying or leading their animals again and again demonstrated the insurmountable barrier between them and their Creator.

But all of that changed when Jesus died on the cross at Calvary, and God illustrated the removal of the sin barrier in dramatic fashion. At the moment when "Jesus cried with a loud voice, and gave up the ghost" (Mark 15:37), the curtain that enclosed the Holy of Holies was torn in two from top to bottom (Mark 15:38). It was God's announcement that the separation was gone and His people could now enter into His presence freely, with Christ as their intermediary. The ideal of the Garden of Eden could at last be fulfilled: God the Father walking in fellowship and peace with the children whom He loves.

The meaning of that supernatural ripping of the temple curtain could not have been clearer. Because of Jesus' death, the path between us and our Heavenly Father is no longer blocked by sin. We are able to "come boldly unto the throne of grace, that we may obtain mercy, and find grace to help in time of need" (Hebrews 4:16). Christ's death on the cross and the bridge it created between us and God means that we can have eternal life in heaven with God and abundant life on earth. It means that our sins are forgiven and that we can walk in His grace, approach Him with boldness in prayer, and serve Him as we seek to advance His kingdom. Because of Calvary, those who trust in Christ are new creations (2 Corinthians 5:17), born again into a wholly new purpose and a life framed by the love of the Father.

Jesus Became Our Mediation

Sinful man is unable to approach God without a mediator, or an intercessor, to represent him. In the Old Testament tabernacle, God set apart the tribe of Levi to act as mediators for the people. When the tabernacle transitioned to the first temple, built by Solomon, and then shifted to renovated temples under Zerubbabel and Herod, the Levites were still the only ones designated to prepare for worship, make the sacrifices, and tend to the holy items in the temple. In order to come to God in any of these worship places, a person had to go through a priest who had the proper lineage and credentials. But like the separation symbolized by the veil, all of that changed with the death of Christ.

Through His death and resurrection, Jesus became the mediator between us and God. Through His intercession, we receive something even better than what the Israelites received in the temple. Hebrews 8:7 tells us that if the rituals of the first law—animal sacrifices, the Levite priests, and the Holy of Holies—could have removed our sin, we would have had no need for a new covenant. But the sanctification rituals of the temple were temporary, and only a holy Mediator could remove our sin once and for all. This new covenant, established by God through the blood of Jesus, is predicated not on the observance of rituals and the obedience of laws, but on God's grace (Hebrews 9:11–14).

After a long line of Levite priests, we have in Jesus God's final Priest for His people. The only person we now have to go through to access God the Father is Jesus Christ. First Timothy 2:5 tells us, "For there is one God, and one mediator between God and men, the man Christ Jesus."

While a building may provide a place for fellowship, worship, and service, we do not need to enter a sanctuary or consult with a minister or priest to commune with God. The Israelites of the Old Testament could seek God only through animal sacrifices and temple rituals, but Jesus suffered and died to introduce a better way. Hebrews 8:6 makes a clear comparison: "But now hath he [Jesus] obtained a more excellent ministry, by how much also he

THE HOLY OF HOLIES · 37

is the mediator of a better covenant, which was established upon better promises." We can build our lives on those better promises because the better covenant has given us holy access to the God who loves, guides, and strengthens us.

Jesus Provided Our Sanctification

The most important ritual observed in the Old Testament temple was animal sacrifice, and this practice provided a vivid picture of the punishment that our sin deserves. "Without shedding of blood is no remission" (Hebrews 9:22), but the blood of animals wasn't truly enough to take care of our sin condition. Every day, observant Israelites and priests watched or participated in grisly animal sacrifices.

At the cross, those present witnessed another grim scene as Jesus bled and died, willingly giving up His life as the final sacrifice for sin. In Hebrews 10:12, we learn that Jesus "offered one sacrifice for sins for ever." The Bible makes it clear that Jesus sacrificed His life once and for all, taking the place of the temple animal sacrifices, by referring to Christ as "the Lamb of God." When John the Baptist saw Jesus approaching him, he made a statement that foreshadowed the fulfillment of God's plan: "Behold the Lamb of God, which taketh away the sin of the world" (John 1:29).

Jesus' walk to the cross was all part of God's plan, but for Jesus, on that dark day, our sanctification came at a price. When He cried out, "My God, my God, why hast thou forsaken me?" (Mark 15:34), Jesus was experiencing the complete alienation from His Father that we were born into because of our sin. He had a taste of spiritual death, and when He gave up His spirit, He also experienced the physical death each of us deserves. As He died, Jesus said, "It is finished" (John 19:30). The price for our sanctification had been paid.

It was by this single sacrifice, the ultimate sacrifice of the Son of God, that God "perfected for ever them that are sanctified" (Hebrews 10:14). The price was paid, and our sanctification was fully accomplished that day on the cross. Because of Jesus, you can be made holy in the eyes of God. This is a free gift of God, and it cannot be earned by good works. As Ephesians 2:8–9 tells us, "For by grace are ye saved through faith; and that not of yourselves: it is the gift of God: Not of works, lest any man should boast."

God with Man

From the time He created man, God has desired to dwell with His people, and the tabernacle and the temple are clear indicators of that desire. The tabernacle and the temple made accommodations for a holy God and sinful man to coexist: separation by way of the veil, mediation by way of the priests, and sanctification by way of the animal sacrifices. Each temple ritual was a step toward the ideal originated in Genesis and the fulfillment of God's promise to Adam and Eve.

The veil, the priests, and the sacrifices all pointed forward to the Deliverer who would deal with sin and death once and for all and reunite God with His people. Jesus Christ, the Son of God, is our Deliverer. By His death and resurrection, He fulfilled God's promise and eliminated the need for the temple. Christianity is the only religion that shows God coming down to earth to redeem His people. With the sacrifice of Christ, we are offered eternal life, peace, purpose, and love everlasting.

The veil has been torn in two. Jesus has eliminated our separation from God, become our mediation, and provided our sanctification. Because of Jesus, you now have an open invitation into the presence of the Most High God.

WORKBOOK

Chapter Three Questions

Question: What is the significance of Jesus comparing Himself to the temple (John 2:18–22)?

_____

_____

_____

_____

_____

_____

_____

_____

_____

_____

Question: What happened to the dividing curtain in the temple when Jesus died? What was the spiritual significance of this event? Why are priests no longer needed as mediators between God and sinners?

_____

_____

_____

_____

_____

_____

_____

_____

_____

_____

_____

Question: Because of Jesus, you can be made holy in the eyes of God. How did Christ accomplish this? What is the difference between the holiness He offers and that of the sacrificial system?

_____

_____

_____

_____

_____

_____

_____

_____

_____

_____

_____

_____

Action: Study Hebrews 4:14–5:9. What does it mean for believers that Jesus is our Great High Priest? Write out five truths about His role as the final and perfect Priest.

_____

_____

_____

_____

_____

_____

_____

_____

_____

_____

CHAPTER FOUR

Not with Hands:
The Holy Spirit and the Church

We have seen Moses oversee the construction of the tabernacle in the wilderness, listened to Solomon's heartfelt prayer as he dedicated the first temple, watched the Babylonians destroy that temple, and witnessed Zerubbabel in his rebuilding project. We have seen the political aspirations of Herod that drove him to double the size of the temple and the Temple Mount in his own renovation.

We stood by as Jesus Christ gave His life on the cross, prompting God to tear the temple veil in two and open the way to the Holy of Holies. The separation was gone. By Christ's blood, He bought our sanctification, and by His resurrection, He became our mediation.

Immediately after Jesus' ascension to heaven, we find the disciples "continually in the temple, praising and blessing God" (Luke 24:53). In the book of Acts, the account of the early Christian Church, believers gathered regularly at the temple, often under Solomon's Portico (Acts 3:11; 5:12). These gatherings were driven by cultural norms and respect for the sanctity of the temple, not a belief that followers of Christ had to submit to temple rituals in order to meet with God.

Because they trusted in what Christ had done on the cross, these believers could gather for meals in someone's home, outside by the lake, or along the road, and anywhere they sought the Lord, they could be ushered into God's presence. But they also took advantage of the temple, the corporate place of worship, to praise God and learn from the Scriptures.

In Acts 7, Stephen, an early Christian convert and the first Christian martyr, stood before a crowd of hostile Jews, preaching Jesus. His sermon recounted God's providence as seen in the lives of the Jewish patriarchs, beginning with Abraham and ending with Solomon, who "built him an house" (Acts 7:47). Stephen respectfully acknowledged that the construction of the tabernacle had followed the command of God. However, he echoed the prayer Solomon offered at the dedication of the temple (1 Kings 8:27), as well as the prophet Isaiah (Isaiah 66:1):

Howbeit the most High dwelleth not in temples made with hands; as saith the prophet, Heaven is my throne, and earth is my footstool: what house will ye build me?
—Acts 7:48–49

An incredible truth is revealed here. God is not confined to any one people or nation, let alone a building. God's presence cannot be contained inside a temple, no matter how grand that structure may be. Even those who lived before the fulfillment of the new covenant grasped God's power and majesty and trusted in His ultimate plan to allow communion between Him and His creation.

Paul understood God's sacrificial plan well, even though he started out as one of the persecutors who participated in Stephen's murder. In his letters to the early Church, Paul presented a new model for the temple—a view of temples that aren't constructed by men at all, but rather ordained by God through the Holy Spirit (1 Corinthians 6:19).

The Church Is the Temple of God

In Paul's first letter to the Corinthians, he addressed a host of problems facing the church in Corinth, such as lawsuits between believers, sexual immorality, and divisions within the body of Christ. In 1 Corinthians 3, Paul focused on the divisiveness that resulted when they rallied around personalities, with some following Paul and others following Apollos. Paul warned them that their testimony and the potential spread of the gospel could be hindered by their disunity.

This situation still happens often in churches today, with Christians identifying so strongly with a specific person, program, ministry, or tradition that they lose sight of the gospel and Christ's call for unity in the body of Christ. Like the Corinthians, we take offense at even the smallest disagreements and create unnecessary divisions that lead to conflict. This discord—most of it born out of our selfishness, which is rooted in sin—keeps the world from experiencing the truth of the gospel.

Paul got right to the heart of things when he asked the Corinthians, "Know ye not that ye are the temple of God, and that the Spirit of God dwelleth in you?" (1 Corinthians 3:16). He was not addressing the church as a building, but as a group of people. God has established the body of Christ as a temple under the new covenant. Solomon and those after him spent countless hours and untold riches making the temple worthy of the living God. Now we, as the body of Christ, must ensure that we are creating a place in which Christ can be glorified.

The temple today is not a building, as well appointed as that building may be. Instead, Scripture tells us that the modern temple is made up of Christ's followers. Every believer is a dwelling place of God, and together we form the corporate temple. Each of us is called to serve that temple by sharing His love with a hurting world and building up His body, the Church. The priesthood isn't limited simply to the tribe of Levi anymore; everyone who trusts in Christ is called to serve His new temple as a priest. As we read in 1 Peter 2:5, "Ye also, as lively stones, are built up a spiritual house, an holy priesthood, to offer up spiritual sacrifices, acceptable to God by Jesus Christ."

The Christian Is the Temple of God

In the same letter, Paul also admonished the Corinthian believers who were caught up in sexual sin. He spent the second half of 1 Corinthians 6 addressing the sexual immorality that was hindering the unity and holiness God intended for the body of Christ. He wrote, "Flee fornication. Every sin that a man doeth is without the body; but he that committeth fornication sinneth against his own body" (1 Corinthians 6:18). Misusing God's gift of sex causes brokenness within a person and also fractures his or her relationships with others.

When we repent of our sin and place our faith in the completed work of Christ on the cross, we experience new birth. We become a new creation, spiritually reborn, and the Holy Spirit takes up residence within us. Second Corinthians 5:17 tells us, "Therefore if any man be in Christ, he is a new creature: old things are passed away; behold, all things are become new." God views us as His children, co-heirs with Christ (Romans 8:17), and as dwelling places of His Holy Spirit. This new state doesn't mean that we will never again struggle with sin, but it does mean that we have a new identity and a new calling to represent Christ with our thoughts and actions. God uses us, His vessels, to reflect His light to a dark world.

The indwelling of the Holy Spirit is one of the great mysteries of the faith, but Scripture is clear that God lives inside of each believer, exerting His grace, providing His comfort, and producing the fruits of His Spirit. In John 14, Jesus referred to the Holy Spirit as the Helper and "the Spirit of truth; whom the world cannot receive," and He reassured His followers that the Spirit would be with us always (John 14:17). We don't have to enter a temple to experience the fullness of God's blessings. The Holy Spirit lives within us; therefore, we are sacred temples of the Lord.

In the Old Testament, God often chose to manifest His presence in specific places and in special ways, as He did in the Garden of Eden, atop Mount Sinai, and within the Holy of Holies. But if we have put our faith in Christ, we can be assured that God's presence is also within each one of us today. The Spirit guides us, comforts us, shows us truth, and even interprets our prayers to the Father when we don't know how to pray on our own (Romans 8:26–27). The Spirit is a precious possession, and we need to guard the temple where He dwells, inside of us.

Speaking to those engaging in sexual sin, Paul asked, "What? know ye not that your body is the temple of the Holy Ghost which is in you, which ye have of God, and ye are not your own?" (1 Corinthians 6:19). Each of us is an individual temple of the Holy Spirit, and that reality brings a different level of accountability to the Christian.

We Are Called to Keep These Temples Pure

Under the new covenant, both the body of Christ and the physical body of the believer are considered temples to be used for the worship and glory of God. Like the Levite priests in the early tabernacle and temple, we are tasked with maintaining the temple in a way that will glorify God and draw others to Him. Proverbs 4:23 reminds us, "Keep thy heart with all diligence; for out of it are the issues of life." How do we guard our hearts and keep God's temple pure? By protecting what we let into our hearts and minds and monitoring what goes out.

Each of us is called to pursue individual discipleship by caring for his or her body as a temple of the Holy Spirit, but we are also responsible for protecting the corporate temple. Within the church, we defile the temple of God when we fall into backbiting, divisions, and petty disputes. Paul warned the church against such things because he recognized the potential damage to the Kingdom of God if the church were to be weakened by sin. Our sin defiles the temple. Then we are no different from the Babylonians who invaded Jerusalem and destroyed the beautiful temple Solomon had built. Just as the Holy of Holies, where God's presence dwelled, was to be kept free of sin, God intends for us to root out the issues in our churches that keep His mission from being fulfilled on the earth today.

When believers gather with unity of purpose and spirit, it is as magnificent as Solomon's temple was in its day, with all its gold and fine furnishings. Because the Church is the temple of God, we must protect its purity and approach it with the awe and reverence worthy of God's dwelling place. That means we are to practice respectful worship, commit to selfless service, and promote teaching that is grounded in truth and relationships in the body that are grounded in honesty, integrity, and unconditional love.

Our calling to keep our temples pure is equally important when we consider our individual bodies. Paul reminded his readers that when they mistreated their bodies sexually, uniting themselves with prostitutes, they were defiling the dwelling place of the Holy Spirit. As 1 Corinthians 6:19 reminds us, we are not our own. We were "bought with a price" (1 Corinthians 6:20), a greater price than billions of dollars of gold and silver. Our temple was purchased with the blood of Jesus. Paul admonished, "Therefore glorify God in your body, and in your spirit, which are God's" (1 Corinthians 6:20). We are the priests of this temple within which the Holy Spirit dwells, and we must embrace the calling to take excellent care of our temples and keep them pure and free from defilement.

In AD 66, in response to a war between Roman soldiers and Jewish nationalists, the invading Roman soldiers killed every Jew in their path and burned the temple to the ground.[6] The spot where the temple had stood remained vacant until AD 685, when construction began on the Muslims' Dome of the Rock, which remains there to this day.[7]

There is no trace of the original temple left in Jerusalem, but we can rejoice that, because of Christ, we no longer need temples to worship and glorify God. Jesus ushered in a new way, clearing the path to His Father so that believers can experience the grace and peace of God anywhere, as long as the Holy Spirit lives within them.

Christ's body, the Church, is now the temple of God. Therefore, we should take seriously our charge to gather for worship (Hebrews 10:25), to bear each other's burdens (Galatians 6:2), and to keep the Church free from petty disputes and divisive sin (Romans 14:1). The Christian's own physical body is also the temple of God, and as such, it should reflect Christ's holiness and purity.

Even if you have never set foot in a temple, you have an open invitation to be a part of a temple and to be a temple yourself. Through God's grace, you can accept Christ and become a dwelling place for God, embracing the abundant life He offers. Is God dwelling within you?

Chapter Four Questions

Question: What does it mean that the Church, the body of believers, is a temple? How can believers protect this temple from destructive influences? What are some of the causes of disunity, and how can you avoid them?

_____

_____

_____

_____

_____

_____

_____

_____

_____

Question: List some of the amazing blessings that the Holy Spirit bestows on each believer. What does it mean for a believer's body to be the temple of the Holy Spirit? In what practical ways can a Christian's body be pure and set apart for worship and service to God?

_____

_____

_____

_____

_____

_____

_____

_____

_____

_____

_____

Question: What happened to the physical temple in Jerusalem? Why does the temple building no longer impact the worship of God?

_____

_____

_____

_____

_____

_____

_____

_____

_____

_____

_____

_____

Action: As believers, we need to protect both our bodies, which are temples of the Holy Spirit, and the Church, which is the corporate temple, from sin. List specific changes that would help you as an individual and your church community as a whole to reflect the purity and holiness of Christ. Pray about taking action in at least some of the areas you have identified.

_____

_____

_____

_____

_____

_____

_____

_____

CONCLUSION

Understanding the Temple:
A Call to Worship

From the temporary tabernacle in the desert to Solomon's grand edifice built in Jerusalem, and from Herod's rebuilt and expanded temple to the New Testament notion of the temple being each believer as well as the Church as a whole, the concept of the temple is crucial at every point in Christian history.

When the Old Testament kings gave tons of gold and sent forth tens of thousands of laborers to the cause of the temple, they did so because they recognized that God is worthy of the highest levels of worship. They wanted to honor God by creating the very best space within which He could dwell. But even though the Old Testament temples were filled with symbolic furnishings and defined by regular acts of worship and sacrifice, they were still only temporary measures on the road to true worship within God's new covenant of grace.

When Jesus came to earth as a man, died on the cross at Calvary, and conquered death by rising again, God tore the heavy temple veil in two (Mark 15:38). There was no longer any barrier between believers and God. Believers could be directly in fellowship with their Creator because of the atonement offered by Christ's shedding of His blood. As children of this new covenant, we can also worship anywhere, never fearing that we might perish in God's holy presence. We take it for granted at times, but we have been allowed complete access to the God of the universe. May we never become too comfortable with Christ's miraculous sacrifice or disregard the gift Jesus gave us at the cross!

We aren't Levite priests, but, as Christians, we are also called to maintain the temple. As "a royal priesthood" of believers (1 Peter 2:9), we must commit ourselves to weeding out disunity and quarreling within the Church, and that process starts with keeping our own hearts pure. The world will only see God's majesty and holiness in the new-covenant temple if we are diligent about honoring Him corporately within the church and individually with our physical bodies. The temple is under our care now, and we can choose either to honor it or to be party to its destruction.

What kind of priest do you want to be? Do you cherish the temple, rejoicing in the fact that you have access to God every day without an earthly intermediary? Do you seek to keep your own body, the temple of the Holy Spirit, pure in every way? Is protecting unity within the Church a top priority for you?

A proper historical understanding of the temple provides an opportunity for each of us to approach worship and discipleship with a new depth and devotion. Enter the temple of Christ with reverence and make Him known to the ends of the earth. Amen!

About the Author

Logan abandoned his surfboard in 2011 in order to move to Provo, Utah, and start a church (crosspointutah.com). The experience has led to his being a regular conference speaker on the topics of church planting and ministry contextualization. He holds a bachelor's degree in Bible and a master's degree in theology. He enjoys hiking with his wife, son, and Boston terrier, though none of them seem to enjoy it as much as he does.

About Sermon To Book

SermonToBook.com began with a simple belief: that sermons should be touching lives, *not* collecting dust. That's why we turn sermons into high-quality books that are accessible to people all over the globe.

Turning your sermon series into a book exposes more people to God's Word, better equips you for counseling, accelerates future sermon prep, adds credibility to your ministry, and even helps make ends meet during tight times.

John 21:25 tells us that the world itself couldn't contain the books that would be written about the work of Jesus Christ. Our mission is to try anyway. Because in heaven, there will no longer be a need for sermons or books. Our time is now.

If God so leads you, we'd love to work with you on your sermon or sermon series.

Visit www.sermontobook.com to learn more.

REFERENCES

Notes

[1] "Temple." Merriam-Webster.com Dictionary. Merriam-Webster. https://www.merriam-webster.com/dictionary/temple.

[2] Dolphin, Lambert. "The Treasure of the House of the Lord." Templemount.org. http://www.templemount.org/TMTRS.html. According to Lambert Dolphin, 100,000 talents of gold is equivalent to 3,750 tons.

"The Value of Gold from a Grain to a Ton." Onlygold. http://onlygold.com/Info/Value-Of-Gold.asp. Based on the value of gold on May 15, 2018, 3,750 tons of gold is worth $141,689,280,000.00.

[3] Jastrow, Morris, Jr., Ira Maurice Price, Marcus Jastrow, and Louis Ginzberg. "Brazen Sea." Jewish Encyclopedia.com. http://www.jewishencyclopedia.com/articles/3659-brazen-sea.

[4] Wood, Leon J. *A Survey of Israel's History*. Revised and enlarged edition. Revised by David O'Brien. Zondervan Academic, 1986.

[5] Price, Randall. *Rose Guide to the Temple*. Rose Publishing, 2012.

[6] "The Romans Destroy the Temple of Jerusalem, 70AD." Eyewitness to History. http://www.eyewitnesstohistory.com/jewishtemple.htm.

[7] "Dome of the Rock: Shrine, Jerusalem." Encyclopaedia Britannica. https://www.britannica.com/topic/Dome-of-the-Rock.

Made in the USA
Columbia, SC
15 August 2020

15579853R00037